The Boston Tea Party

The Boston Tea Party

Dennis Brindell Fradin

Marshall Cavendish
Benchmark

New York

Dedication

For my granddaughter, Shalom Amelia Richard, with love

Marshall Cavendish Benchmark
99 White Plains Road
Tarrytown, NY 10591
www.marshallcavendish.us

Text and maps copyright © 2008 by Marshall Cavendish Corporation
Maps by XNR Productions

Library of Congress Cataloging-in-Publication Data

Fradin, Dennis B.
The Boston Tea Party / Dennis Brindell Fradin.
p. cm. — (Turning points in U.S. history)
Includes bibliographical references and index.
ISBN-13: 978-0-7614-2035-4
1. Boston Tea Party, 1773—Juvenile literature. I. Title. II. Series.
E215.7.F73 2007
973.3'115—dc22
2006025344

Photo research by Connie Gardner

Cover Photo: Time Life Pictures/Stringer/Getty
Title Page: Dave Bartruff/CORBIS

The photographs in this book are used by the permission and through the courtesy of: *Corbis:* 6,14,16,19,24; *The Granger Collection:* 10,12,13,22,30,34,36; *Getty:* MPI Stringer, 9; North Wind Pictures: 18,20,26,29.

Time Line: Dave Bartruff/CORBIS

Editor: Deborah Grahame
Publisher: Michelle Bisson
Art Director: Anahid Hamparian

Printed in Malaysia
1 3 5 6 4 2

Contents

This engraving shows the arrival of early colonists at Jamestown, Virginia.

CHAPTER ONE

Britain Rules the Thirteen Colonies

England settled Virginia, its first permanent American **colony**, in 1607. More English colonies soon followed. By 1733 England ruled thirteen American colonies: Virginia, Massachusetts, New Hampshire, New York, Connecticut, Maryland, Rhode Island, Delaware, Pennsylvania, North Carolina, New Jersey, South Carolina, and Georgia.

Now and then the colonists and their British rulers had disagreements. For the most part, though, Britain ruled its thirteen colonies peacefully. When called upon, the Americans came to the aid of their Mother Country, as they nicknamed Britain.

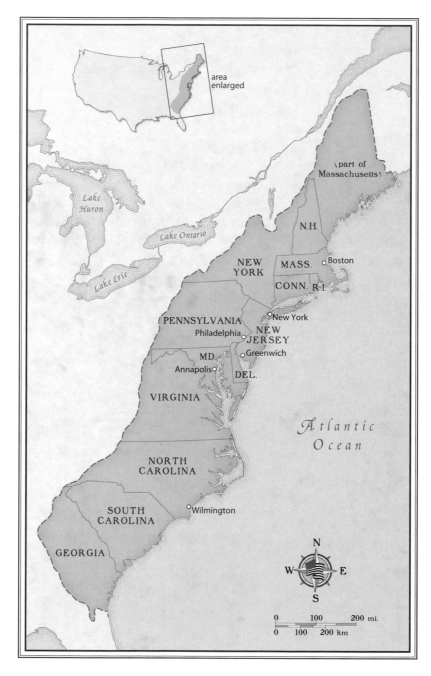

The original thirteen American colonies settled between 1607 and 1733.

The French and Indian War (1754–1763) was waged by Britain and France for control of North America.

Between 1754 and 1763 Britain and France fought a war for control of North America. This conflict is called the French and Indian War because thousands of Native Americans sided with France. Thousands of American colonists fought for Britain. Thanks partly to the colonists' help, England won the war.

Angry colonists are shown gathering in public and denouncing the Stamp Act.

CHAPTER TWO

Trouble Brews

England won the war, but there was a problem. The French and Indian War had been very costly. The Mother Country owed 158 **million** pounds—its largest national debt up to that time. This amount would equal many **billions** of American dollars today.

How would the British government pay its debts? British lawmakers argued that the war had made the thirteen colonies safe from the French. Therefore, the colonists should help foot the bills. In 1765 Britain's **parliament** (government) passed the Stamp Act, the first major tax on the colonists. Americans had to buy special tax stamps to be placed on documents such as wills, newspapers, marriage licenses, and diplomas.

The colonists were outraged. They should be *thanked* for helping England win the war, not *taxed*, they complained. Americans throughout the thirteen colonies held meetings and street **rallies** to protest the Stamp Act.

An Emblem of the Effects of the STAMP O! the fatal Stamp

A warning about the Stamp Act printed as a cartoon in *The Pennsylvania Journal*, 1765.

Several people in Boston, Massachusetts, led the protest against the new tax. "Taxation without representation is **tyranny**!" Boston's James Otis declared. Colonists from New Hampshire to Georgia repeated this slogan. It meant that since Parliament contained no Americans, it had no right to tax its colonies. Bostonian Samuel Adams wrote letters to newspapers to attack the Stamp Act. Adams also organized a group of three hundred men to fight the new tax. He called them the Sons of Liberty.

Samuel Adams

Samuel Adams was born in Boston, Massachusetts. He failed at just about everything he did for years. Only the quest for American independence claimed his full attention. He and Virginia's Patrick Henry both favored independence by 1765. They are considered the first prominent Americans to do so. Using false names, Adams sent hundreds of letters to newspapers complaining about British injustice. Often he answered his own letters. This made it seem like all of Boston was aflame over British taxes. For his efforts in planning the Boston Tea Party and other events that sparked the Revolution, Adams became known as the Father of American Independence.

Samuel Adams (1722–1803)

Citizens of New York and Boston rioted against the Stamp Act. Some groups protested violently by tarring and feathering stamp agents, and by destroying stamps in bonfires.

Under Adams's direction, the Sons of Liberty turned Boston into America's most **rebellious** town. The Sons of Liberty destroyed homes of British officials. They rioted in the streets. Partly because of the violence in Boston, Parliament **repealed** the Stamp Act in 1766.

Britain was not done trying to tax the Americans. In 1767 Parliament passed the Townshend Acts. These new laws taxed paint, tea, lead, paper, and glass brought into the colonies. Again Americans protested, especially Boston's Sons of Liberty. Again Britain backed down—but not completely this time. In 1770 Parliament repealed all the Townshend taxes except one. The Mother Country kept the tax on tea to show Americans that they could not always have their way.

In December 1773 about 1,000 people met in New York and decided to turn back any British ships carrying tea. In this engraving they are shown listening to a reading of the Tea Act.

CHAPTER THREE

The Tea Act

For about three years, Americans paid little attention to the tax on tea. Many of them did not drink British tea anyway. Instead they broke the British law by **smuggling** in Dutch tea.

Then, in May 1773, Parliament passed the Tea Act. This new law cut the price of tea nearly in half, while keeping the tax on it. The Tea Act was meant to achieve three goals. First, it would lure Americans to buy tea from the East India Company, a British firm with a large supply of tea on its hands. Second, it would prevent Americans from smuggling Dutch tea. Finally, it would show the world that Americans cared more about saving money than about "taxation without representation."

Besides not buying British tea, patriotic colonial women spun their own cloth to avoid using cloth imported from Britain.

The colonists were not as greedy or as easily fooled as the British believed, however. They gathered at meetings and agreed not to buy British tea even though it was cheaper. Women and girls also protested, which was unusual in an era when females usually kept away from politics. They formed groups called the Daughters of Liberty and signed pledges promising not to buy British tea. Instead they used mint leaves and raspberries to make tea for their families. They called their homemade beverages liberty tea.

The British were still determined to sell their tea in America. They sent shiploads of East India Company tea to American ports. The *Dartmouth* arrived in Boston Harbor on November 28, 1773. The *Eleanor* and the *Beaver* reached Boston soon after. Together the three ships held 342 chests of British tea—but they would not hold them for long.

This drawing shows the interior of the Old South Meeting House.

CHAPTER FOUR

"Boston Harbor a Teapot Tonight!"

Samuel Adams, the leader of Boston's Sons of Liberty, posted armed guards along the waterfront. They made sure that British officials did not try to bring the tea ashore. Meanwhile, Adams formed a plan to destroy the tea. He kept it so secret that, even today, the details are unclear.

We do know that on Thursday, December 16, 1773, Boston had its biggest public gathering up to that time. About seven thousand people crowded into and around the Old South Meeting House. The townspeople sent a message to Governor Thomas Hutchinson, who ruled

John Hancock

John Hancock was born in Braintree, Massachusetts. In 1764, at the age of twenty-seven, Hancock inherited most of his uncle's fortune. Although most rich Americans favored Britain in Revolutionary days, Hancock sided with the colonists. John donated so much money to the American cause that his friends joked, "Samuel Adams writes the letters and John Hancock pays the postage." In 1775 Hancock was elected president of the Continental Congress. As such, he became the first man to sign the Declaration of Independence in 1776. Hancock later served as governor of Massachusetts for eleven years.

John Hancock (1737–1793)

Massachusetts for King George III of Britain. The message was simple: order the tea ships away from Boston. The governor's answer arrived at about six o'clock that evening: "No!"

Adams then stood up and addressed the thousands of angry Bostonians. "This meeting can do nothing more to save the country!" he shouted. These words were a **prearranged** signal to about fifty men, disguised as Indians, whom Adams had stationed at the church entrance.

"Boston Harbor a teapot tonight!" shouted the "Indians," waving their hatchets in the air.

As the church emptied, John Hancock, another rebel leader, yelled out: "Let every man do what is right in his own eyes!" Some members of the crowd decided to help the "Indians" destroy the tea—by now everyone had figured out the purpose of the hatchets.

By the time the mob reached the waterfront, it numbered about 150 men. Paul Revere was one of them, but the identities of most of the others remain unknown to this day. The men boarded the three ships.

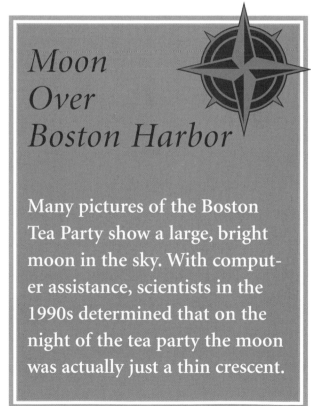

Moon Over Boston Harbor

Many pictures of the Boston Tea Party show a large, bright moon in the sky. With computer assistance, scientists in the 1990s determined that on the night of the tea party the moon was actually just a thin crescent.

Dramatic drawings of the Boston Tea Party, such as this one, are common, but the actual dumping of the tea and tea chests was quiet and orderly.

By the light of lanterns and torches, they smashed open the 342 chests. The men then dumped all of the tea into Boston Harbor as a crowd of **spectators** watched.

It took the men about three hours to open the chests and to throw the tea overboard. When their mission was complete, the men marched off to the tooting of a **fife**. As the men made their way home, British navy admiral John Montagu heard them joking about how they had turned Boston

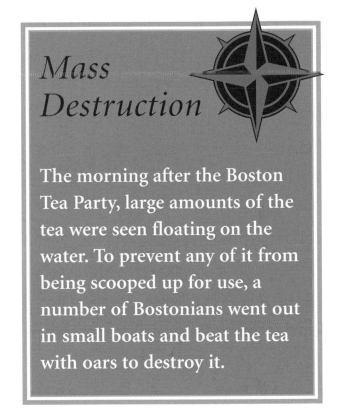

Mass Destruction

The morning after the Boston Tea Party, large amounts of the tea were seen floating on the water. To prevent any of it from being scooped up for use, a number of Bostonians went out in small boats and beat the tea with oars to destroy it.

Harbor into a teapot. Sticking his head out a window, Admiral Montagu said, "Well, boys, you've had a fine, pleasant evening for your **caper**. But mind, he who dances must pay the fiddler."

The expression "paying the fiddler" meant that the men would have to pay for what they had done. One of the tea dumpers shouted back, "Oh, never mind, Admiral. Just come out here, and we'll settle the bill in two minutes!"

News about the tea dumping spread quickly. The event became known as the Boston Tea Party. It triggered a new series of events that led to American independence.

TOWN OF BOSTON WITH SEVERAL SHIPS OF WAR IN THE HARBOUR

In 1774 British warships entered Boston Harbor to make sure the seaport remained closed.

CHAPTER FIVE

The Rebellion Spreads

England decided to punish Boston for its tea party. Punishment would make the Bostonians more obedient. It also would prevent other colonists from becoming rebellious—or so the British thought.

Parliament passed the **Coercive** Acts in the spring of 1774. Thomas Gage, a British general backed by a large army, was appointed to govern Massachusetts. In addition, starting June 1, no ships would be permitted to enter or leave Boston Harbor until the colonists paid for the destroyed tea. Boston was a seaport, so this would cost many Bostonians their jobs. It might even lead to widespread starvation in the town.

On May 12, 1774, leaders from the Boston area gathered to decide what to do. Their meeting was a crucial moment in American history. If the leaders decided to pay for the tea, the **revolutionary** flame might die out.

Costly Party

In today's U.S. money, the tea destroyed at the Boston Tea Party had a value of roughly one million dollars.

Instead, the leaders took a bold stand. They vowed that Boston would not pay for the tea. As threatened, Boston's port was closed on June 1, 1774. Thousands of Bostonians were thrown out of work. Still, the townspeople refused to pay for the tea.

Samuel Adams, who had planned the famous tea party, asked other colonies for help. "An attack on the liberties of one colony is an attack upon the liberties of all," Adams wrote. Paul Revere and other riders delivered Adams's letters to leaders across colonial America.

The other colonies responded. On June 1, 1774, patriots in Philadelphia, Pennsylvania, tolled their church bells in sympathy for Boston. Virginia legislators took Thomas Jefferson's advice and spent the day fasting (not eating) and praying. Fellow colonists provided something

Paul Revere

Boston native Paul Revere (1735–1818) attended school until age thirteen and then became a silversmith. He was also a gifted artist. He created engravings and political cartoons supporting the Americans in their struggle with England. Revere became best known as the rebels' chief messenger. His first ride of Revolutionary times was a more than 300-mile journey to bring the news of the Boston Tea Party to New York and Philadelphia. He later made more than twenty other rides, including his famous ride to Lexington and Concord. During the Revolution, Revere made cannons for George Washington's army. Revere, who wore his Revolutionary War uniform for the rest of his life, lived to the age of eighty-three.

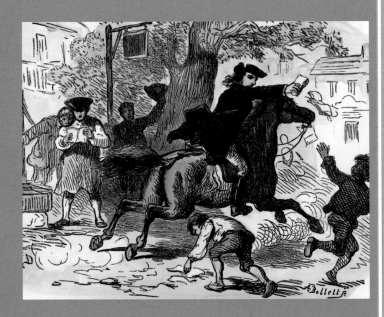

Paul Revere delivered handbills for the Sons of Liberty.

An amusing British drawing shows women in North Carolina signing a resolution not to drink British tea.

else Bostonians needed: food. The nearby towns of Salem and Marblehead let Boston use their ports. Food was shipped to these towns and taken by cart overland to Boston. People in New York, Rhode Island, Maryland, North and South Carolina, and other colonies made generous donations. The corn, rye, beef, sugar, fish, bread, pork, rice, and money they sent helped the Bostonians survive.

The events in Boston inspired other tea parties. On the night of April 22, 1774, New York City patriots dumped eighteen boxes of British tea into the water. In October 1774 Americans in Annapolis, Maryland, forced a man to burn his own ship carrying British tea. South Carolinians threw a shipload of tea into Charleston Harbor on November 1, 1774. In December 1774 patriots dressed as Indians broke into a cellar in Greenwich, New Jersey. They seized some British tea and burned it.

Women sometimes took part in these acts of destruction. In March 1775 women in Wilmington, North Carolina held a tea party. They burned British tea.

A colonist leaves home to join the local militia marching off to war.

CHAPTER SIX

A New Nation Is Born

Punishing Boston for its tea party did not make Americans more obedient, as Britain had hoped. In fact, the opposite happened. Americans were more united and determined than ever in opposing the Mother Country.

At the suggestion of Samuel Adams and Pennsylvania's Benjamin Franklin, American leaders met in Philadelphia in the fall of 1774. They held the First **Continental Congress** to discuss the troubles with England. Among other suggestions, Congress told the colonies to form **militias** in case war broke out. These emergency troops came into play a few months later.

In April 1775 Massachusetts governor Thomas Gage decided to crush the rebels in the Boston area once and for all. Gage planned to strike a double blow at the rebels. His troops would capture Samuel Adams and John Hancock, who had taken refuge outside Boston in Lexington, Massachusetts. Gage's troops would then seize military supplies stored by the rebels at nearby Concord, Massachusetts.

Thanks to Paul Revere's most famous ride, Adams and Hancock were warned that the British were coming. The two American leaders fled Lexington in the nick of time. Had they been captured, Adams and Hancock might have been executed.

Thomas Gage (1721–1787) was commander in chief of the British army in America from 1763 to 1775, when he was recalled to England.

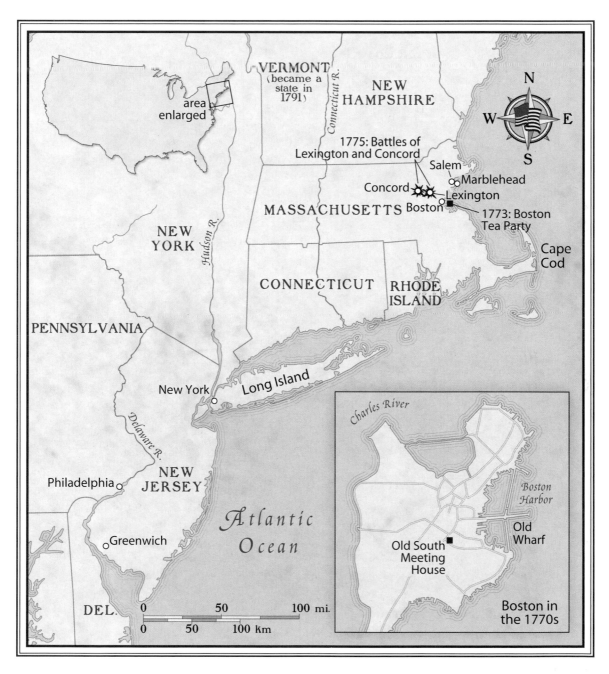

This map shows where key events mentioned in this book occurred.

British soldiers are shown retreating after the Battle of Concord.

The British troops reached Lexington at dawn on April 19, 1775. The Lexington militiamen, some of whom were known as **minutemen**, fought the redcoats. The Americans lost the Battle of Lexington. Later that day, however, they defeated the British at the Battle of Concord.

The Battles of Lexington and Concord marked the start of the American Revolution. The next year, in July 1776, Americans declared their independence from Britain. The Americans finally won the war in 1783. The Boston Tea Party had helped spark a major conflict. That conflict was over, and the United States took its place among the nations of the world.

Glossary

billions—One billion equals a thousand million (1,000,000,000).

caper—A prank, escapade, or illegal act.

coercive—Forcing people to obey.

colonies—Settlements built by a country beyond its borders.

Continental Congress—A body of lawmakers that governed the American colonies before the creation of the United States Congress.

fife—A small musical instrument in the flute family.

militias—Emergency troops.

million—One million equals a thousand thousand (1,000,000).

minutemen—Revolutionary militiamen who claimed they could get ready to fight the British at a minute's notice.

parliament—The lawmaking body of Britain and many other countries.

prearranged—Set up ahead of time.

rallies—Large meetings to create enthusiasm or support.

rebellious—Tending to resist authority, rules, or power.

repealed—Canceled something or brought it to an end.

revolutionary—Relating to the overthrow of a government.

smuggling—Transporting something illegally.

spectators—Onlookers.

tyranny—Unjust and oppressive power.

Timeline

1607—Virginia, England's first permanent American colony, is settled

1765—Britain's parliament passes the Stamp Act, sparking American protests

1620—Pilgrims settle in Massachusetts, England's second American colony

1766—Parliament repeals the Stamp Act

1733—Georgia, the last of England's thirteen American colonies, is founded

1767—Britain passes the Townshend Acts, taxing the colonists

1754–1763—American colonists help Britain win the French and Indian War

1770—Britain repeals all the Townshend taxes except the tax on tea

1607   *1766*   *1770*

1773—May 10: Parliament passes the Tea Act, which slashes the price of tea while keeping the tax on it; **December 16:** Americans destroy a huge amount of British tea at the Boston Tea Party

1775—April 19: Revolutionary War begins at Lexington and Concord in Massachusetts

1776—Declaration of Independence is approved on July 4

1774—Parliament passes the Coercive Acts to force Bostonians into obedience; other colonies send food and money to aid Boston; several colonies hold their own tea parties

1973—Two-hundredth anniversary of the Boston Tea Party

1773   *1776*   *1973*

Further Information

BOOKS

Dolan, Edward F. *The Boston Tea Party*. New York: Marshall Cavendish, 2002.

Draper, Allison Stark. *The Boston Tea Party: Angry Colonists Dump British Tea*. New York: Rosen, 2001.

Furstinger, Nancy. *The Boston Tea Party*. Mankato, Minnesota: Capstone Press, 2002.

Hull, Mary E. *The Boston Tea Party in American History*. Berkeley Heights, NJ: Enslow, 1999.

WEB SITES

For information on the tea party from the Boston Tea Party Ship &
    Museum
http://www.bostonteapartyship.com/

For an eyewitness account of the Boston Tea Party
http://www.historyplace.com/unitedstates/revolution/teaparty.htm

For a variety of information about the Boston Tea Party
http://www.kidport.com/RefLib/UsaHistory/AmericanRevolution/TeaParty.htm

Bibliography

Canfield, Cass. *Samuel Adams's Revolution*. New York: Harper & Row, 1976.

Fischer, David Hackett. *Paul Revere's Ride*. New York: Oxford University Press, 1994.

Fowler, William M. Jr. *The Baron of Beacon Hill: A Biography of John Hancock*. Boston: Houghton Mifflin, 1980.

Hall-Quest, Olga W. *Guardians of Liberty: Sam Adams and John Hancock*. New York: Dutton, 1963.

Labaree, Benjamin Woods. *The Boston Tea Party*. New York: Oxford University Press, 1964.

Colonial Massachusetts: A History. Millwood, N.Y.: KTO Press, 1979.

Lewis, Paul. *The Grand Incendiary: A Biography of Samuel Adams*. New York: Dial, 1973.

Wells, William V. *Life and Public Services of Samuel Adams*. Boston: Little Brown, 1866 (reprinted 1969).

Index

Page numbers in **boldface** are illustrations.

About the Author

Dennis Fradin is the author of 150 books, some of them written with his wife, Judith Bloom Fradin. Their recent book for Clarion, *The Power of One: Daisy Bates and the Little Rock Nine*, was named a Golden Kite Honor Book. Another of Dennis's recent books is *Let It Begin Here! Lexington & Concord: First Battles of the American Revolution*, published by Walker. The Fradins are currently writing a biography of social worker and antiwar activist Jane Addams for Clarion and a nonfiction book about a slave escape for National Geographic Children's Books. Turning Points in U.S. History is Dennis Fradin's first series for Marshall Cavendish Benchmark. The Fradins have three grown children and three young grandchildren.